EMMANUEL JOSEPH

The Quiet Titans, Billionaires Who Redraw Maps and Rewrite the Story of Industries

Copyright © 2025 by Emmanuel Joseph

All rights reserved. No part of this publication may be reproduced, stored or transmitted in any form or by any means, electronic, mechanical, photocopying, recording, scanning, or otherwise without written permission from the publisher. It is illegal to copy this book, post it to a website, or distribute it by any other means without permission.

First edition

This book was professionally typeset on Reedsy.
Find out more at reedsy.com

Contents

1. Chapter 1: The Architects of Change — 1
2. Chapter 2: The Tech Visionaries — 3
3. Chapter 3: Masters of Finance — 5
4. Chapter 4: The Healthcare Innovators — 7
5. Chapter 5: The Green Pioneers — 9
6. Chapter 6: Retail Revolutionaries — 11
7. Chapter 7: Media Moguls — 13
8. Chapter 8: The Education Entrepreneurs — 15
9. Chapter 9: Real Estate Reimaginers — 17
10. Chapter 10: Transportation Trailblazers — 19
11. Chapter 11: The Quiet Philanthropists — 21
12. Chapter 12: Energy Innovators — 23
13. Chapter 13: The Data Defenders — 25
14. Chapter 14: The Agri-Tech Innovators — 27
15. Chapter 15: The Social Media Giants — 29
16. Chapter 16: The Silent Disruptors — 31
17. Chapter 17: The Legacy Builders — 33

1

Chapter 1: The Architects of Change

In the realm of modern industries, some individuals stand as titans, their influence far-reaching, yet their names often remain unsung. These billionaires are not just wealthy—they are architects of change, redesigning the landscapes of their respective fields with quiet determination. Unlike the flashy moguls who court media attention, these quiet titans operate behind the scenes, making seismic shifts that redefine our everyday experiences. They possess a unique vision and relentless drive, pushing the boundaries of innovation and setting new standards for excellence. Their impact is profound, felt in the products we use, the services we rely on, and the very fabric of our daily lives. These architects of change are not driven by the pursuit of fame or fortune, but by a deep-seated desire to make a difference.

Their stories often begin with humble beginnings, where curiosity and passion laid the foundation for their future success. Through sheer determination and an unwavering belief in their ideas, they have overcome obstacles and navigated the complexities of their respective industries. These quiet titans are masters of strategy, able to anticipate market shifts and adapt their approaches to stay ahead of the curve. They are risk-takers, willing to invest in uncharted territories and embrace the unknown. Their ability to see opportunities where others see challenges has propelled them to the forefront of their fields.

One defining characteristic of these architects of change is their commitment to sustainability and social responsibility. They understand that true success is measured not just by financial gains, but by the positive impact they can create. Whether it's through philanthropy, environmental initiatives, or community development projects, these billionaires are dedicated to leaving a lasting legacy. They recognize that their influence extends beyond their businesses and strive to create a better world for future generations. Their actions inspire others to follow suit, driving a wave of change that transcends industries and borders.

In this book, we will delve into the lives and achievements of these remarkable individuals. We will explore the innovations they have introduced, the challenges they have faced, and the transformations they have sparked. Through their stories, we will gain a deeper understanding of what it takes to be a quiet titan in today's ever-evolving world. Join us on this journey as we uncover the untold stories of those who have redrawn maps and rewritten the story of industries, shaping the world as we know it.

2

Chapter 2: The Tech Visionaries

Silicon Valley is home to a unique breed of billionaires—tech visionaries who have transformed the way we live, work, and communicate. From the dawn of personal computing to the rise of the internet, these individuals have been at the forefront of technological innovation. Their contributions have not only created new industries but have also dismantled traditional ones, pushing boundaries and challenging the status quo.

These tech visionaries are driven by a passion for innovation and a relentless pursuit of excellence. They possess a deep understanding of technology and its potential to change the world. Through their companies, they have introduced groundbreaking products and services that have revolutionized entire industries. Their ability to anticipate future trends and adapt to changing market dynamics has set them apart as leaders in their field.

One such visionary is a pioneer in the world of personal computing. Starting with a small garage operation, this individual turned their passion for technology into a global empire. Their innovative approach to software development and user-friendly interfaces transformed the way people interact with computers. Through their vision, personal computing became accessible to millions, democratizing technology and empowering individuals around the world.

Another tech visionary has redefined the concept of connectivity. Through their relentless pursuit of innovation, they created a social media platform that has connected billions of people across the globe. This platform has not only changed the way we communicate but has also become a powerful tool for social and political movements. Their vision of a connected world has reshaped our society, fostering new forms of collaboration and engagement.

In the world of e-commerce, another titan has revolutionized the way we shop. By leveraging the power of the internet, they created an online marketplace that offers unparalleled convenience and access to a vast array of products. Their innovative business model has disrupted traditional retail, setting new standards for customer experience and redefining the future of commerce. Through their vision, they have created a platform that empowers small businesses and entrepreneurs, driving economic growth and opportunity.

These tech visionaries are not only shaping the present but also paving the way for the future. Their contributions to fields such as artificial intelligence, renewable energy, and space exploration are setting the stage for the next wave of technological advancements. They are driven by a desire to solve complex problems and create a better world for future generations. Through their work, they continue to push the boundaries of what is possible, inspiring others to dream big and pursue their own visions.

3

Chapter 3: Masters of Finance

In the world of finance, there are those who wield their power not through ostentatious displays of wealth, but through strategic acumen and foresight. These financial wizards have reshaped global markets, steering economies with a deft hand. Their influence extends beyond boardrooms and trading floors, impacting the lives of millions. Through savvy investments and innovative financial instruments, they have rewritten the story of wealth creation and distribution.

These masters of finance possess an unparalleled understanding of market dynamics and economic trends. They have an innate ability to identify opportunities and make strategic decisions that yield significant returns. Their success is not the result of luck but of meticulous research, analysis, and a keen sense of timing. They are adept at navigating the complexities of financial markets, leveraging their expertise to create value and drive economic growth.

One such financial titan is known for their ability to predict market trends with remarkable accuracy. Through their hedge fund, they have consistently delivered impressive returns, outperforming the market and setting new benchmarks for success. Their investment philosophy is rooted in rigorous analysis and a deep understanding of economic fundamentals. They have a knack for identifying undervalued assets and positioning themselves to capitalize on market inefficiencies.

Another master of finance has made their mark through innovative financial instruments. By pioneering new investment products, they have expanded the range of opportunities available to investors. Their contributions have democratized access to capital markets, allowing individuals from all walks of life to participate in wealth creation. Through their vision, they have created a more inclusive financial system that empowers individuals and promotes economic mobility.

In the realm of private equity, another titan has reshaped industries through strategic acquisitions and investments. By identifying companies with high growth potential and providing them with the necessary resources and expertise, they have driven transformative change. Their approach to value creation extends beyond financial metrics, focusing on operational improvements, innovation, and long-term sustainability. Through their work, they have revitalized struggling businesses and created new opportunities for growth.

These masters of finance are not content with simply amassing wealth; they are driven by a desire to make a meaningful impact. Many of them are active philanthropists, using their resources to support causes that align with their values. Through their charitable foundations, they address pressing social issues, from education and healthcare to poverty alleviation and environmental conservation. Their philanthropy is strategic and impactful, aimed at creating lasting change and improving the lives of those in need.

4

Chapter 4: The Healthcare Innovators

Healthcare is another arena where quiet titans make their mark. These billionaires have transformed the industry through groundbreaking research, innovative treatments, and the establishment of global health initiatives. Their contributions have led to life-saving advancements and improved the quality of healthcare worldwide. They are driven by a vision of a healthier future, one where access to medical care is universal and disease is no longer a death sentence.

These healthcare innovators are at the forefront of medical research, pushing the boundaries of what is possible. Through their funding and support, they have enabled scientists and researchers to explore new frontiers in medicine. Their investments in biotechnology and pharmaceutical companies have led to the development of new drugs and therapies that have saved countless lives. They are champions of innovation, continuously seeking new ways to address complex health challenges.

One such innovator is a pioneer in the field of genetic research. By unlocking the secrets of the human genome, they have paved the way for personalized medicine. Their work has revolutionized the treatment of diseases, allowing for tailored therapies that target specific genetic mutations. Through their vision, they have brought hope to patients with rare and previously untreatable conditions, transforming the landscape of medical care.

Another healthcare titan has focused their efforts on global health initiatives. Through their foundation, they have launched programs that address the most pressing health issues facing underserved populations. From vaccination campaigns to efforts to eradicate diseases like malaria and polio, their work has had a profound impact on global health. They are driven by a belief that everyone, regardless of where they live, should have access to quality healthcare.

In the realm of medical technology, another innovator has introduced cutting-edge devices that have revolutionized patient care. Their innovations range from advanced imaging systems to minimally invasive surgical tools, improving outcomes and reducing recovery times. Through their work, they have empowered healthcare professionals to deliver better care and improve the quality of life for patients around the world.

These healthcare innovators are also committed to addressing the social determinants of health. They understand that factors such as education, housing, and nutrition play a crucial role in overall well-being. Through their philanthropic efforts, they support initiatives that address these underlying issues, promoting health equity and social justice. Their vision of a healthier future extends beyond the confines of hospitals and clinics, encompassing the broader determinants of health and well-being.

5

Chapter 5: The Green Pioneers

Environmental sustainability has found its champions among the ranks of quiet billionaires. These individuals are not only investing in green technologies but are also advocating for policies that promote environmental responsibility. From renewable energy projects to sustainable farming practices, their efforts are reshaping industries and steering the world toward a more sustainable future. They are proving that economic success and environmental stewardship can go hand in hand.

One prominent green pioneer is known for their work in renewable energy. By investing in solar and wind power, they have significantly contributed to reducing our reliance on fossil fuels. Their initiatives have not only lowered carbon emissions but have also created jobs and stimulated economic growth in various regions. Their vision is a world where clean energy is the norm, and they are dedicated to making that a reality through continuous innovation and advocacy.

Another green titan has revolutionized the agriculture industry with sustainable farming practices. By promoting organic farming, reducing pesticide use, and implementing advanced irrigation techniques, they have increased crop yields while minimizing environmental impact. Their work has inspired a new generation of farmers to adopt sustainable methods, ensuring that future generations will have access to healthy, nutritious food. Their commitment to environmental stewardship extends beyond their own enterprises, as they advocate for policies that support sustainable agriculture on a global scale.

In the realm of green technology, another pioneer has introduced innovative solutions to address environmental challenges. From electric vehicles to energy-efficient appliances, their products have set new standards for sustainability. Through their vision, they have demonstrated that technological advancement and environmental responsibility are not mutually exclusive. Their efforts have paved the way for a future where technology is harnessed to protect and preserve the planet.

These green pioneers are also active in promoting environmental education and awareness. They understand that creating a sustainable future requires a collective effort, and they are dedicated to inspiring others to join the cause. Through their philanthropic initiatives, they support environmental organizations, fund research, and engage in public outreach campaigns. Their legacy is not just in the technologies they develop or the policies they advocate for, but in the movement they inspire, driving global action toward a more sustainable and resilient world.

6

Chapter 6: Retail Revolutionaries

In the realm of retail, there are visionaries who have changed the way we shop. From the creation of global e-commerce giants to the reinvention of brick-and-mortar stores, these billionaires have revolutionized the retail experience. Their innovations have made shopping more convenient, personalized, and accessible, reshaping consumer behavior and setting new standards for the industry.

One such retail revolutionary is credited with creating an e-commerce platform that has become a household name. By leveraging the power of the internet, they have made it possible for consumers to shop from the comfort of their homes, accessing a vast array of products at the click of a button. Their platform offers personalized recommendations, fast shipping, and seamless customer service, setting a new benchmark for online shopping. Their vision of a borderless marketplace has connected sellers and buyers from around the world, driving economic growth and creating new opportunities.

Another retail titan has reimagined the traditional brick-and-mortar store. Through innovative store designs, immersive experiences, and cutting-edge technology, they have transformed the way consumers interact with physical retail spaces. Their stores offer not just products, but experiences that engage all the senses, creating a deeper connection between the brand and the customer. Their approach has breathed new life into retail, proving that physical stores can thrive in the digital age.

In the world of luxury retail, another visionary has disrupted the industry by making high-end fashion more accessible. By creating a platform that offers designer clothing and accessories at affordable prices, they have democratized luxury fashion. Their business model, which includes partnerships with top designers and a focus on sustainability, has resonated with consumers who seek quality and value. Through their vision, they have expanded the reach of luxury brands and redefined what it means to shop for high fashion.

These retail revolutionaries are also committed to social responsibility. They understand that their success is intertwined with the well-being of the communities they serve. Through philanthropic initiatives, they support causes such as education, healthcare, and environmental conservation. Their commitment to giving back is a testament to their belief that businesses can be a force for good, driving positive change in society.

7

Chapter 7: Media Moguls

The media landscape has been transformed by the silent efforts of certain billionaires. Through strategic acquisitions, investments in content creation, and the development of new distribution channels, they have redefined the way we consume information and entertainment. Their influence reaches into our homes, shaping public opinion and cultural narratives with a subtle, yet profound impact.

One notable media mogul has built an empire through the strategic acquisition of media companies. By identifying undervalued assets and investing in their growth, they have created a conglomerate that spans television, film, and digital media. Their vision is to provide high-quality content that entertains, informs, and inspires. Through their leadership, they have set new standards for content creation and distribution, influencing the media landscape for generations to come.

Another media titan has revolutionized the way we consume news and information. Through the development of a digital platform that aggregates content from various sources, they have made it easier for consumers to access reliable and diverse news. Their platform uses advanced algorithms to personalize content, ensuring that users receive news that is relevant to their interests. Their commitment to journalistic integrity and transparency has earned them the trust of millions, making their platform a go-to source for news and information.

In the realm of entertainment, another mogul has made a significant impact by producing groundbreaking films and television shows. Through their production company, they have championed diverse voices and stories, bringing underrepresented narratives to the forefront. Their work has not only entertained audiences but has also sparked important conversations about social issues. Their vision is to use the power of storytelling to drive cultural change and promote understanding and empathy.

These media moguls are also committed to supporting the next generation of content creators. Through mentorship programs, scholarships, and funding for independent projects, they are nurturing new talent and promoting diversity in the media industry. Their efforts are creating opportunities for aspiring writers, directors, and journalists to share their stories and make their mark on the world. Their legacy is not just in the content they produce, but in the platform they provide for others to tell their own stories.

8

Chapter 8: The Education Entrepreneurs

Education is another field where quiet titans have left an indelible mark. These individuals have founded institutions, developed innovative educational technologies, and championed policies that promote access to quality education. Their efforts have expanded opportunities for millions, breaking down barriers and democratizing knowledge. They are paving the way for a future where education is not a privilege but a fundamental right.

One education entrepreneur has transformed the landscape of online learning. Through the creation of a comprehensive e-learning platform, they have made education accessible to anyone with an internet connection. Their platform offers courses from top universities and industry experts, covering a wide range of subjects. Their vision is to provide lifelong learning opportunities, empowering individuals to acquire new skills and knowledge throughout their lives. Their work has revolutionized education, making it more flexible, affordable, and inclusive.

Another titan in the education sector has focused on early childhood education. By developing innovative curricula and educational tools, they have improved the quality of education for young children. Their programs emphasize holistic development, incorporating not just academics but also social, emotional, and physical well-being. Through their efforts, they have provided children with a strong foundation for lifelong learning and success.

Their vision is to ensure that every child has access to high-quality early education, regardless of their background or circumstances.

In the realm of higher education, another entrepreneur has founded a network of universities that prioritize innovation and entrepreneurship. Their institutions offer cutting-edge programs that prepare students for the challenges of the 21st century. By fostering a culture of creativity and critical thinking, they are equipping students with the skills and mindset needed to thrive in a rapidly changing world. Their vision is to create a global network of institutions that drive positive change and contribute to the advancement of society.

These education entrepreneurs are also advocates for policy changes that promote access to quality education. They understand that systemic change is necessary to address the inequities in the education system. Through their advocacy work, they support policies that increase funding for education, improve teacher training, and promote equity and inclusion. Their efforts are creating a more just and equitable education system that benefits all students, regardless of their socioeconomic status.

9

Chapter 9: Real Estate Reimaginers

The real estate industry has seen its share of quiet titans who have reimagined urban landscapes and transformed communities. Through visionary development projects, they have revitalized cities, created sustainable living environments, and addressed housing shortages. Their work is not just about building structures; it's about creating spaces that enhance the quality of life and foster community.

One such real estate reimaginer is known for their innovative approach to urban development. By combining modern architecture with sustainable design principles, they have created vibrant mixed-use communities that integrate residential, commercial, and recreational spaces. Their projects prioritize green spaces, walkability, and accessibility, promoting a healthier and more connected urban lifestyle. Their vision is to create cities that are not only functional but also beautiful and inclusive.

Another titan in the real estate sector has focused on affordable housing. Through strategic partnerships with governments and non-profit organizations, they have developed housing solutions that cater to low-income families. Their initiatives include the construction of high-quality, affordable housing units and the provision of supportive services such as job training and financial education. Their work has provided stability and opportunity for countless families, transforming lives and strengthening communities.

In the realm of luxury real estate, another visionary has set new standards for opulence and innovation. By developing iconic buildings that push the boundaries of design and engineering, they have created landmarks that define city skylines. Their projects incorporate cutting-edge technologies, sustainable practices, and luxurious amenities, offering residents an unparalleled living experience. Through their vision, they have redefined what it means to live in a modern, luxury environment.

These real estate reimaginers are also committed to social and environmental responsibility. They understand that their projects have a lasting impact on the communities they serve, and they strive to create positive change. Through their philanthropic efforts, they support initiatives that promote education, healthcare, and environmental conservation. Their legacy is not just in the buildings they create, but in the vibrant, sustainable communities they help to build.

10

Chapter 10: Transportation Trailblazers

Transportation has been revolutionized by billionaires who have envisioned new ways of moving people and goods. From electric vehicles to private space exploration, these trailblazers are pushing the boundaries of what is possible. Their innovations are not only making transportation more efficient and sustainable but are also opening up new frontiers for exploration and commerce.

One prominent transportation trailblazer is known for their work in electric vehicles. By developing cutting-edge electric cars that combine performance, sustainability, and affordability, they have disrupted the automotive industry. Their vision is to create a future where clean transportation is the norm, reducing our dependence on fossil fuels and mitigating the impact of climate change. Through their relentless pursuit of innovation, they have set new standards for the industry and inspired a global shift toward electric mobility.

Another transportation visionary has turned their sights to the skies, pioneering private space exploration. Through their aerospace company, they have developed reusable rockets that significantly reduce the cost of space travel. Their ambitious goals include establishing human settlements on other planets and making space travel accessible to the masses. Their work is opening up new possibilities for scientific research, commercial ventures, and the future of humanity in space.

In the realm of urban transportation, another titan has revolutionized the way we navigate cities. By developing a comprehensive network of shared mobility services, including ride-sharing, bike-sharing, and electric scooters, they have made urban transportation more convenient, affordable, and sustainable. Their vision is to create smart cities where residents can easily access a variety of transportation options, reducing traffic congestion and improving air quality.

These transportation trailblazers are also committed to addressing the broader challenges of mobility and accessibility. Through their philanthropic initiatives, they support projects that promote transportation equity, ensuring that underserved communities have access to reliable and affordable transportation options. Their efforts are creating a more inclusive and connected world, where everyone has the opportunity to move freely and pursue their goals.

11

Chapter 11: The Quiet Philanthropists

Philanthropy is a realm where many billionaires quietly make a significant impact. Through generous donations and the establishment of foundations, they support causes that address pressing global issues. Their philanthropy is strategic and impactful, often focusing on long-term solutions rather than short-term fixes. They are driven by a desire to leave a lasting legacy that benefits humanity as a whole.

One such quiet philanthropist is known for their unwavering commitment to education. By funding scholarships, building schools, and supporting educational programs, they have provided opportunities for countless individuals to pursue their dreams. Their vision is to create a world where education is accessible to all, regardless of socioeconomic background. Through their efforts, they have empowered individuals to break the cycle of poverty and achieve their full potential.

Another philanthropic titan has focused on healthcare. Through their foundation, they support medical research, fund hospitals, and provide access to life-saving treatments for underserved populations. Their work has led to significant advancements in the fight against diseases such as malaria, HIV/AIDS, and cancer. Their vision is a world where everyone has access to quality healthcare, and their contributions have brought hope and healing to millions.

In the realm of environmental conservation, another philanthropist has made a profound impact by supporting initiatives that protect and preserve our planet. Their efforts include funding research on climate change, supporting conservation projects, and advocating for sustainable practices. Through their vision, they have helped to raise awareness about the importance of environmental stewardship and inspired others to take action. Their work is creating a more sustainable and resilient future for generations to come.

These quiet philanthropists are also champions of social justice. They understand that true progress requires addressing the root causes of inequality and injustice. Through their philanthropic initiatives, they support organizations that promote human rights, advocate for marginalized communities, and work to create a more just and equitable society. Their legacy is not just in the financial contributions they make, but in the positive change they inspire and the lives they transform.

12

Chapter 12: Energy Innovators

The energy sector has been reshaped by billionaires who are driving the transition to renewable energy sources. Through investments in solar, wind, and other clean technologies, they are reducing our reliance on fossil fuels and mitigating the impacts of climate change. Their work is not just about generating profits; it's about creating a sustainable energy future for generations to come.

One notable energy innovator has made significant strides in the development of solar power. By investing in large-scale solar farms and advancing photovoltaic technology, they have increased the efficiency and affordability of solar energy. Their vision is to harness the power of the sun to provide clean, renewable energy to communities around the world. Through their efforts, they have made solar power a viable alternative to traditional energy sources, reducing carbon emissions and promoting environmental sustainability.

Another titan in the energy sector has focused on wind power. Through the development of innovative wind turbines and the establishment of offshore wind farms, they have harnessed the power of the wind to generate electricity. Their projects have not only provided a clean energy source but have also created jobs and stimulated economic growth in coastal regions. Their vision is a future where wind power plays a central role in the global energy mix, driving the transition to a low-carbon economy.

In the realm of energy storage, another innovator has introduced groundbreaking solutions to address the intermittency of renewable energy sources. By developing advanced battery technologies, they have created efficient and scalable energy storage systems that enable the integration of renewable energy into the grid. Their work is paving the way for a more resilient and reliable energy infrastructure, ensuring that clean energy can be available whenever it is needed.

These energy innovators are also advocates for policy changes that support the transition to renewable energy. They understand that achieving a sustainable energy future requires collaboration between governments, businesses, and communities. Through their advocacy efforts, they promote policies that incentivize renewable energy development, reduce greenhouse gas emissions, and support environmental conservation. Their vision is a world where clean energy is the norm, and their contributions are driving us toward that future.

13

Chapter 13: The Data Defenders

In an age where data is the new oil, there are billionaires who have taken on the role of data defenders. They are developing technologies and policies to protect our digital lives and ensure that data privacy is maintained. Their efforts are crucial in a world where cyber threats are ever-present and the misuse of data can have far-reaching consequences.

One such data defender is known for their work in cybersecurity. Through the development of advanced security protocols and encryption technologies, they have created solutions that safeguard sensitive information from cyberattacks. Their vision is to create a secure digital environment where individuals and businesses can operate without fear of data breaches. Their efforts have set new standards for cybersecurity, ensuring that our digital infrastructure is resilient and protected.

Another titan in the field of data privacy has focused on creating platforms that give users control over their personal information. By developing tools that allow individuals to manage their data and make informed choices about its use, they have empowered users to take charge of their digital identities. Their vision is a world where data privacy is a fundamental right, and their work is driving the industry toward greater transparency and accountability.

In the realm of artificial intelligence, another innovator is addressing the ethical implications of data usage. By developing AI systems that prioritize fairness, transparency, and accountability, they are ensuring that these technologies are used responsibly. Their efforts include creating frameworks for ethical AI development and advocating for policies that protect individuals from the potential harms of AI. Their vision is to harness the power of AI in ways that benefit society while safeguarding human rights.

These data defenders are also active in promoting data literacy and education. They understand that protecting our digital lives requires not just technological solutions but also informed and aware users. Through their philanthropic initiatives, they support programs that teach digital literacy, cybersecurity skills, and data privacy awareness. Their legacy is not just in the technologies they create, but in the empowered and informed digital citizens they help to cultivate.

14

Chapter 14: The Agri-Tech Innovators

Agriculture is another industry that has been transformed by quiet billionaires. Through the development of agri-tech solutions, they are addressing challenges such as food security, sustainability, and efficiency. Their innovations are helping to feed a growing global population while minimizing the environmental impact of farming practices.

One such agri-tech innovator is known for their work in precision agriculture. By leveraging technologies such as drones, sensors, and data analytics, they have created systems that optimize crop management. Their solutions provide farmers with real-time information on soil health, weather conditions, and crop performance, enabling them to make data-driven decisions. Their vision is to create a more efficient and sustainable agricultural system that maximizes yields while minimizing resource use.

Another titan in the agri-tech sector has focused on developing sustainable farming practices. By promoting techniques such as crop rotation, agroforestry, and organic farming, they have reduced the environmental impact of agriculture. Their initiatives have also improved soil health, increased biodiversity, and enhanced resilience to climate change. Their vision is to create a regenerative agricultural system that restores ecosystems and supports long-term food security.

In the realm of agricultural biotechnology, another innovator has introduced groundbreaking solutions to address food production challenges.

Through the development of genetically modified crops that are resistant to pests, diseases, and environmental stresses, they have increased agricultural productivity and reduced the need for chemical inputs. Their work is helping to ensure that we can feed a growing global population while protecting the environment.

These agri-tech innovators are also advocates for policies that support sustainable agriculture and food security. They understand that achieving these goals requires collaboration between governments, businesses, and communities. Through their advocacy efforts, they promote policies that incentivize sustainable farming practices, support research and innovation, and ensure that everyone has access to nutritious food. Their vision is a world where agriculture is sustainable, resilient, and capable of meeting the needs of future generations.

15

Chapter 15: The Social Media Giants

The rise of social media has been spearheaded by billionaires who have created platforms that connect billions of people worldwide. These platforms have revolutionized communication, commerce, and culture, creating new opportunities and challenges. The influence of these social media giants is profound, shaping public discourse and personal relationships in ways that were unimaginable a few decades ago.

One notable social media giant has built an empire through the creation of a platform that connects people from all walks of life. By providing a space for individuals to share their thoughts, experiences, and ideas, they have transformed the way we communicate. Their platform has become a powerful tool for social and political movements, enabling users to organize, advocate, and effect change. Their vision is to create a more connected and informed world, where everyone has a voice.

Another titan in the social media industry has focused on visual content. Through the development of a platform that allows users to share photos and videos, they have revolutionized the way we consume and create visual media. Their platform has become a hub for creativity, self-expression, and community building. Their vision is to empower individuals to tell their stories and connect with others through the power of visual storytelling.

In the realm of professional networking, another innovator has created a platform that connects professionals from around the world. By providing a space for individuals to showcase their skills, build their networks, and find job opportunities, they have transformed the way we navigate our careers. Their platform has become an essential tool for professional development and career advancement. Their vision is to create a world where everyone has the opportunity to succeed and thrive in their chosen field.

These social media giants are also committed to addressing the challenges associated with their platforms, such as misinformation, privacy concerns, and online harassment. Through their efforts, they are developing tools and policies to protect users, promote accurate information, and create a safer online environment. Their vision is to harness the power of social media for good, creating platforms that are not only engaging but also responsible and ethical.

16

Chapter 16: The Silent Disruptors

Across various industries, there are silent disruptors who challenge the status quo and drive change. These billionaires are not content with incremental improvements; they seek to revolutionize industries and create entirely new paradigms. Their disruptive innovations have far-reaching impacts, often leading to the rise of new markets and the decline of old ones.

One such silent disruptor has made a significant impact in the field of transportation. By developing a revolutionary mode of transport that combines speed, efficiency, and sustainability, they have disrupted traditional transportation systems. Their vision is to create a future where transportation is seamless, sustainable, and accessible to all. Their work is paving the way for new possibilities in urban mobility and long-distance travel.

Another titan in the realm of financial technology has introduced innovations that challenge traditional banking and finance. Through the development of blockchain technology and digital currencies, they have created new ways of conducting transactions, storing value, and accessing financial services. Their vision is to democratize finance, making it more transparent, secure, and inclusive. Their disruptive innovations are transforming the financial landscape, offering new opportunities for individuals and businesses alike.

In the world of entertainment, another silent disruptor has redefined the way we consume and create content. By developing a platform that offers on-demand streaming services, they have changed the way we watch movies and television shows. Their vision is to provide a personalized and convenient entertainment experience, giving users access to a vast library of content at their fingertips. Their work has disrupted traditional media distribution models, setting new standards for the industry.

These silent disruptors are not only focused on creating innovative products and services but also on addressing broader societal challenges. They understand that true disruption requires a holistic approach that considers social, environmental, and economic impacts. Through their philanthropic initiatives and advocacy efforts, they support causes that align with their values and contribute to positive change. Their legacy is not just in the disruptions they create, but in the new possibilities they inspire.

17

Chapter 17: The Legacy Builders

In the end, the quiet titans of industry are not just building businesses; they are building legacies. Their contributions extend beyond their lifetimes, shaping the future in ways that are both profound and enduring. They are the architects of a new world, where innovation, sustainability, and social responsibility are the cornerstones of progress. Through their quiet, yet powerful efforts, they are rewriting the story of industries and leaving a lasting impact on the world.

These legacy builders understand that true success is measured not just by financial gains, but by the positive impact they can create. They are driven by a vision of a better world, one where businesses play a central role in addressing global challenges. Their work is characterized by a commitment to innovation, sustainability, and social responsibility, setting new standards for what it means to be a successful entrepreneur.

One such legacy builder is known for their dedication to environmental conservation. Through their investments in renewable energy, sustainable agriculture, and conservation projects, they have made significant contributions to protecting our planet. Their vision is a world where economic success and environmental stewardship go hand in hand. Their work has inspired others to take action, driving a global movement toward sustainability.

Another titan in the realm of philanthropy has focused their efforts on education and healthcare. By funding scholarships, building schools, and supporting medical research, they have provided opportunities and improved the quality of life for countless individuals. Their vision is a world where everyone has access to quality education and healthcare, regardless of their background or circumstances. Their contributions have created a lasting legacy, transforming lives and communities.

In the world of technology, another legacy builder has introduced innovations that have changed the way we live, work, and communicate. Through their work, they have made technology more accessible, user-friendly, and impactful. Their vision is to harness the power of technology to create a more connected and empowered world. Their legacy is not just in the products they create, but in the opportunities they provide for others to innovate and thrive.

In a world where the loudest voices often dominate, there exists a select group of billionaires who quietly transform industries and shape our future. **"The Quiet Titans: Billionaires Who Redraw Maps and Rewrite the Story of Industries"** delves into the lives and achievements of these influential yet unassuming individuals. From tech visionaries to green pioneers, from healthcare innovators to education entrepreneurs, this book explores the profound impact they have had on our world.

Through seventeen captivating chapters, discover how these titans of industry have revolutionized technology, finance, healthcare, retail, media, transportation, and more. Learn about their visionary approaches, strategic investments, and unwavering commitment to sustainability and social responsibility. Their stories reveal the power of innovation and the importance of creating a lasting legacy that benefits humanity.

"The Quiet Titans" is not just a celebration of success but a testament to the transformative power of quiet determination and visionary thinking. It offers a unique perspective on the individuals who, without fanfare, have redrawn maps and rewritten the story of industries, leaving an indelible mark on our lives and our future.

www.ingramcontent.com/pod-product-compliance
Lightning Source LLC
LaVergne TN
LVHW020459080526
838202LV00057B/6049